Critical Acclaim

"Gervais weaves an anecdotal tapestry whose threads continue to knit through the reader's imagination long after the book has been put away."

Canadian Literature

"...for him, the act of making a poem or telling a story is an act of faith, so that observances of the commonplace become moments of transcendent epiphany and insight, rather than merely journalistic jottings or diaries"

The Oxford Companion to Canadian Literature.

"The best of Marty Gervais' work creates an engaging tension between the ordinary surfaces of life and the underlying pathos...

The Globe and Mail

"...Gervais doesn't strike me as a particularly "literary" poet. I mean his concerns are with human feelings, laughter, what happens inside the brain when certain lights are turned on. He strikes me as honest...I mean there's no phoniness...no pretensions..."

Al Purdy, Governor General's Award Winner

"Over the span of a fifty-year career, in poems that are delightful and memorable, Marty Gervais is one of the finest poetic voices in Canada. His powerful and cleat reportage, his keen eye for the unusual in the everyday, and his delight in our humanity affirm Gervais as an essential chronicler of our beautiful souls."

Bruce Meyer, renowned Author and Poet, CBC Broadcaster

A New Dress Every Day

*Poems in
My Mother's Voice*

Marty Gervais

mosaicPRESS

Library and Archives Canada Cataloguing in Publication

Title: A new dress every day : poems in my mother's voice /
         Marty Gervais.

Names: Gervais, C. H. (Charles Henry), 1946- author.

Identifiers: Canadiana (print) 20210169214
             Canadiana (ebook) 20210169249

ISBN 9781771615648 (softcover) ISBN 9781771615655 (PDF)
ISBN 9781771615662 (EPUB) ISBN 9781771615679 (Kindle)

Classification: LCC PS8563.E7 N49 2021
                DDC C811/.54—dc23

Published by Mosaic Press, Oakville, Ontario, Canada, 2021.

MOSAIC PRESS, Publishers
www.Mosaic-Press.com
Copyright © Marty Gervais

Printed and bound in Canada

Mosaic Press
1252 Speers Road, Units 1 & 2, Oakville, Ontario, L6L 5N9
(905) 825-2130 • info@mosaic-press.com • www.mosaic-press.com

A Selection of Book Titles by Marty Gervais

Non-fiction

The Rumrunners (Firefly Books), 1980
Seeds in the Wilderness: Profile of Religious Leaders. (Quarry Press, 1994).
From America Sent: Letters to Henry Miller. (Quarry Press, 1995).
Reno (A Novel), (Mosaic Press, 1996)
My Town: Faces of Windsor (Biblioasis Books), 2006
The Rumrunners: A Scrapbook of Prohibition (Biblioasis Books), 2007
Ghost Road and Other Forgotten Stories of Windsor (Biblioasis Books) 2012

Poetry

A Sympathy Orchestra (Fiddlehead Books) 1970
Poems for American Daughters (Porcupine's Quill) 1976
The Believable Body (Fiddlehead Books) 1979
Up Country Lines (Penumbra Books) 1979
Into A Blue Morning: Selected Poems, with introduction by Al Purdy (Hounslow Press) 1982
Letters from the Equator. Penumbra Press, 1986.
Scenes from the Present: New Selected Poems. Penumbra Press, 1991
Playing God. Mosaic Press, 1994..
Tearing Into a Summer Day. Mosaic Press, 1996.
The Science of Nothing (Mosaic Press, 2000).
To Be Now: New and Selected Poems (Mosaic Press, 2003).
Table Manners (Selected and New Poems 2014-2018 (Mosaic Press, 2018)
Nine Lives: A Reunion in Paris (Urban Farmhouse Press, 2020)

Table of Contents

These poems were inspired by the stories my mother told me about her childhood and growing up on a farm outside of Pointe-aux-Roches, deep in the heart of Ontario's Essex County. Hers was a life dominated by religion and superstition and storytelling. This is a glimpse of Marie-Anne Mineau and a time and a place and a culture long forgotten but deeply rich in what it has to offer.

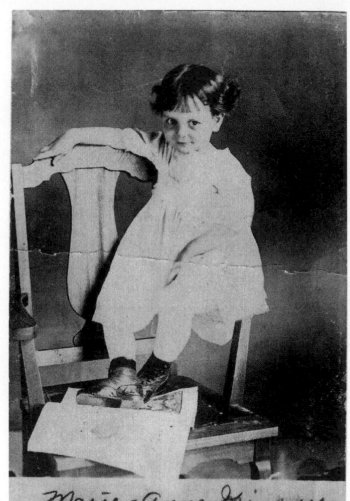

Marie-Anne Mineau

Preface
By Micheline Maylor

In the 70's, when I was growing up in Windsor, Ontario, Marty Gervais was a legend. It was the time of newspapers as a daily ritual accompanied by coffee and cigarettes (not me, I was too young). A time when adults would read aloud articles and say, "Hey, Miche, what dyathink of this?" Often times those stories were written by the journalist Marty Gervais.

It was not until I grew up and met Marty that we realized my great-parents and Marty's mother came from the same town: Pointe-aux-Roche. Given that they were born about ten years apart, and the population was a whooping 375, it was quite likely they knew of each other, and they understood one another's town. They would have gone to the same church. It was a French speaking town, with its odd accent known as Muskrat French, due to the blending of cultures and old French brought from settlers. At the time, Stoney Point, Ontario, as it's known in English, was a quiet agricultural village with one church, one store, and a great big beach, and a couple of cars. Marty's family was Settler-French and, no doubt, they all farmed in the lush and humid seasons, on land that amply provides: walnuts, cherries, corn, wheat, peaches, tomatoes, squash, beans, you name it.

Once Marty and I started talking, we found eerie similarities sprung from this sliver of land that is so small, if you blink you miss it. We both heard tales of the seventh son of the seventh son, Archille Baillargeon, who was a

known healer; we'd both heard of poltergeists and ghost
stories that have caused the living to evacuate homes, and
we both had our own experiences of paranormal around
those parts; and there was Windsor. This was a time when
cars were a brand-new invention and Windsor was a boom-
ing, wild metropolis with financial and cultural opportu-
nity, but a world away, even from Lakeshore; Detroit was
another country, and a big city with an entirely different
culture. It was a long way from Pointe-aux-Roches.

Marty likes to say that "history is real life stories, right
under our noses that connect to the way we live and behave
today." *A New Dress Every Day* is a portrait of his mother in
that time as she moved from that pastoral farmland to the
big town of Windsor. My great-grandmother, too, moved
to Windsor, not speaking for a while in order to disguise
her low accent and worked in a laundry, then a pillow fac-
tory.

Women of this time, including Marty's mother, may
have been forgotten. At the time, women were called pos-
sessions: wife of Gervais. My own Mimi was Alphonse's
wife.

In this tender portrait, Marty Gervais brings forth
the woman behind the kitchen door. The mother, the
woman, and her motives, experience, and struggles. Her life
becomes a real-life story of a young, displaced farm girl,
of a certain time, moving to the big city. It is a tender and
accurate glimpse of domesticity of the early-mid twentieth
century, tinted with the beliefs of the time, and the realities
of south Ontario in the 1930's-50's. This is a real tribute
to the women behind the history, and those whose pasts we
have built on. It's Marty's love story to his mother.

POEMS

What Comes from Silence

What comes from sitting here so high
up in a black walnut tree hidden behind
all that swarms with silence but for
the ease of wind that lightly sweeps
across the stretch of fields

I see barns and fences and farmhouses
and men working in the open air and
from time to time a truck passing by
on straight roads that run from the village
and down to the lake and the lighthouse

I am a young farm girl climbing high
aloft all the hush of an ordinary day
searching for words to sing its praise
complete its welcome and find that moment
of grace in being alone

Baptism

I am told I was a month old —
a warm humid day in late September
just before the harvesting of soybeans
and I was told how the priest kept coughing
and turning away and apologizing
and my mother worried over
whether I might get sick
like a cousin of hers
who lost a four-month-old to influenza

She said my eyes never left focus
on the priest whose face convulsed in spasms
—hands damp with holy water blessed me
In the name of the Father, the Son, the Holy Spirit

And my eyes, dreamy blue idly scanned
the sweeping arches of the sanctuary—
its magnificent angels swarmed in celebration
of this moment in a rural church
whose steeple towered over the flat open farmland

I am told my mother believed I saw angels
real festive spirits that soared above me and singing
She swore to the family gathered all around
that she pictured this reflected in my eyes —
angels hovering so close she could nearly
reach out and hold them still
but the priest's coughing might
have scared them away

Now, as an old woman in a hospital bed
with a crucifix above the doorway
I wonder whatever happened
to those angels, and why they are not here
to comfort my wide-awake blue eyes

What My Mother Said

I only know what my mother said
that it was late October —
a balmy Fall day after the harvest
and I was asleep in the pram
and my mother covered me up
and left me in the sunlight
while she hung out sheets and towels
on a sagging and wilting clothesline
that ran from the house to a shed

When she went back to check on me
I was gone — a two-month-old infant
vanishing into thin air

and my mother spun around
and spun around again
eyes wild and frantic —
but there was nothing in the flat open fields
but a barn and a henhouse and beyond
a grove of black walnut trees

I had disappeared —
I only know what my mother said
how it wasn't until nightfall that
she found me at a nearby farm
at the far reaches
among a caravan of travelers
broken-down wagons and dogs and bonfires
and she had to barter for me
hand over eggs and bread and corn
till finally they placed me into my mother's arms

and she carried me, briskly marching
a mile and half back to the farm
clutching me close to her for all the world

I only know what my mother said

Fields of Ghosts

As a girl of not more than five
I imagined these ghosts of the field rising
in the early morning from the long sweep
of cornfields and wondered at their misty
apparition waking to this sun-warmed land

heard stories of them returning and finding
a way to tell us of their deep longing
to set things right, earn our blessings
and so, I prayed for these ghosts
that swarmed from the fields with the sun

heard tales of long dead aunts
uncles and grandparents who long ago
gathered for picnics after Mass in late spring
in the black walnut grove back of the barn
and now they clamber all the while

for my attention as I find my way
to the farmhouse window to catch them as they stir
in the stilled gracefulness of dawn, I spy
how their deep shadows chase away the glare
with a plea for my forgiveness

Moving to the City

The house in Windsor my father rented
had an indoor toilet and a porcelain tub
and a curved verandah out front
and he worried less in 1927
working now every day at the Ford Foundry
and life was good in the city

Still, I missed the schoolhouse in Stoney Point
its narrow windows, lopsided planked floor
but mostly the language that I knew
— after a while it was better I didn't speak at all
I had only ever heard English maybe at the gas station
or someone stopping by the farm for directions

I didn't mind other girls poking fun at me
— shy, skinny and long dresses and clunky shoes
and a barber's haircut, or even when
they mocked my fractured English
but when the priest told my teacher I was illiterate
I told him I didn't need English to speak to God

Church Suppers in the Great Depression

I normally offered to help out
at church suppers at Annunciation
that drew cousins and uncles and aunts
and families from all over Tilbury North
25 cents for turkey and creamed corn
and butterscotch pies
but if I mopped floors and served tables
I could fill my plate after most had left
heading home to nearby farms and villages
and I'd sit with the volunteers
in the church basement

but I stopped going when I was 14
started making excuses, busying myself
with hauling water, gathering eggs
filling the wood box
and I missed the dances —
waltzes and jigs and two-steps
and the shrill sound of violins

I missed it because one night
after everyone else had left
my sister said a cousin who
after scrubbing the kitchen down
and switching off the church lights
and feeling entirely good about herself
told her uncle, who had patiently waited
to take her back to the farm
that she was ready, and when

he was helping her on with her coat
he abruptly pressed her up against a wall
and started kissing her —

trembling and frightened, she did nothing
she let him — numb in that moment
in all the purity of God's darkness

The Photographer

A strip of afternoon light on the door
at the front of the house
muted and warm, a fleeting dream

I was wearing a gingham dress
ivory coloured ankle socks, my hair in braids
not quite 16 and it was early spring

That day my father was angry
peering up over the newspaper
from the high back pine rocking chair
in the middle of the big kitchen
woolen socks and feet resting near the wood stove
eyes steely and blue, a voice certain and steady

I lied about doing my chores
I lied about my older sister swearing
I also lied to my mother but worst of all
I was too coy with the photographer
who stopped by the farm
in hope of taking a family portrait
I had no business flirting, no business moving
the way I did, hips and legs swaying
when he set up his camera

I protested, I was shy, I didn't know how to stand
I didn't know how to pose but I liked it
when the man directed me: *I like the way you look*
like the way you move...Do that again... Yes ...
That's good...That's perfect... Now straighten up
and lift your chin, dear... Yes, that's really good ...Now hold it ...

I spotted my father out of the corner of my eye
striding across the dark field, and hollering at the man
to pack up his things and scowling at me
and gestured for me to get back to the house

Later, I told him I was sorry
I hated apologizing

But I lied — a month later when I went
to fetch the mail by the road, there was a letter
addressed to me — from that man's studio in Windsor

I stood leaning against the crooked mailbox
puzzling over a photograph of me posing

there I was — skinny legs, long eyelashes
high cheekbones, that bright gingham dress
forever feeling that moment
and the sun on my shoulders

It didn't look at all like me

The Faith Healer

There was the faith healer
an uncle who came by Sundays after Mass
driving up in his sprawling Studebaker
and stayed for breakfast even offering
to accompany me to the henhouse
where I would pluck eggs from under the hens
the warmth of them collected in my wide apron

and he'd talk to me the whole time
mostly asking questions —
or telling me *Stay close to God*

I never knew what to say
because it made no sense when
cousins and aunts and other uncles
died of influenza or smallpox

I saw them all laid out in farmhouse parlours
Why couldn't he save them?
Why didn't he help? Did God let him down?
I never asked him
I listened, I watched, I waited —
sometimes my focus strayed to a detail
a loose button on his jacket
long fingernails, a crooked front tooth
his voice dissolving into the wallpapered kitchen

I swore he could heal people —
I watched him run his long narrow hands
over my sister's right forearm
that was bright red with a rash

that she had all summer long
and my uncle prayed, eyes
rolling up to the heavens asking
for this unsightly bloom on her arm
to fade away, disappear

A day or two later it vanished

I swore he could —
until my little brother fell feverish
and my uncle kept promising
for weeks on end
but he never came out to the farm

Now every Sunday after Mass
I pause at my brother's gravestone
praying still, to stay closer to God

My German Grandmother

I can't be sure it had anything to do with me
for there were times when I sat upright
in the darkness of the big room
with the west windows and saw the moon
drifting like a scared ghost
among dark shapes of barns and silos
and I wondered about her —

the grandmother who died years ago
and why she persisted in frightening us
and why the priest couldn't do something
why all the holy water and incense and rosaries
couldn't stop cupboard doors from slamming
why the windows rattled, and the house trembled
and the wallpaper peeled and why now
I was awake sitting on my bed fearing her

I swear I saw her one night hovering
at the far end of the hallway near the stairs
and felt a chill on the back of my neck
and when I spoke, a picture above the doorway
fell to the floor, spun around and crashed again

There were times when reading late
and the pages of my book
began lifting and turning rapidly
and moments when I woke abruptly
to sounds of footsteps near my bed

I can't be sure, but the last time I saw her
she was standing in the window —
silhouetted in the light of an August moon
and I stepped out of bed, bare feet
moving boldly past her and opened
wide the shutters, and I swear
she slipped away and I felt the house
shudder and grow quiet —
and she was gone

Half Brother

His mother had passed away
and the family left him in the care
of my mother —

a new brother to me
and my sister — a son my parents
had lost, and I was five when
he came to live with us

and we called him our half brother
and he grew up in our house
even after his father re-married

I helped him with schoolwork
sitting side by side in the kitchen
at night after supper but soon found
he was better with arithmetic
better at geography than me

and he grew up with our surname
though there never was any paperwork

No one bothered in those days
— he was never adopted
and he never gave it a thought
till the day he was getting married

and now the woman he was marrying
was taking a name she never dreamed of

First Visit to Point Pelee

I heard about a botanist
who had trampled its woods and filled cases
with weeds and bugs and plants
and kept detailed logs on weather
and set up camps at the tip
fighting off its fierce and wicked storms
his tents blown down and billowing away
into the depths of the lake

I read about the Point in the papers
this crazy spit of land
twenty-six miles from the farm
that jutted deep and out into Lake Erie
like a slender finger — a paradise
for pecans and oranges
where cactus and northern Tamaracks
thrived side by side along with
two hundred species of bird

and so, when I was invited
to join my sister and ride in
her boyfriend's 1932 Ford V8 with
its flashy colour-keyed wheels and white walls
we felt pretty special, giggling all the way
along dirt roads, finally reaching the Point
motoring past cottagers and beaches
and parked cars from as far away as Ohio
the sight of Lake Erie dazzling in the heat

and we picnicked on the west side —
sporting wide-brimmed sun hats
and fanning out a bright tablecloth to hold
wicker baskets brimming with sandwiches and apples
and my sister's boyfriend brought some wine
something I had never seen except at church

and maybe she drank a little too much
or maybe it was merely innocent giddiness
but as the afternoon faded and my sister
and her boyfriend were still swimming
in the late summer light
I felt uneasy, watching them
worried about her silliness

and so, I busied myself, tidying up
the tablecloth, fussing over picnic baskets
trying to make everything right — that's
when I heard my sister's voice
rising in the darkening landscape
where land and sky are one and mute
and saw her boyfriend frantically grasping
to pull her back from the grips of the undertow

then silence, and only the point of land
reaching out into the graying bleakness of a day
that had started so promising

when finally, I spotted the two of them—
emerging almost in slow motion
at the very edge of the sweeping tip
struggling to stand, then falling
and standing, hovering like an apparition

I couldn't move from where I was sitting
I couldn't speak — and I didn't

I rode in silence all the way back to the farm

For days, I did not talk to my sister

The Promise

I'll buy you flowers
I'll buy you candy
I'll take you dancing
Marry me

This is what he told me
the moment he met me

I was barely 18 —
a farmer's daughter
working as a housekeeper
for his cousin's family

Said he was in love with me
and wouldn't let it go
mischievously chased me
when I made the beds
swept the floors
or washed the windows

and later we both laughed about it

Still, he pestered me with a thousand questions
about my parents, siblings, anything
really just to keep the conversation going

I coyly ignored him, dodged him
scorned his advances
I wouldn't have any of it —
until he finally promised

I'll buy you a new dress every day
Marry me

Two Brides Two Months Apart

We wanted husbands
but it was Rose who would go first
two months before me but at his church
not ours in Stoney Point
— she was already showing
and needed to be married quickly

My father refused to give her away
or let me be a bride's maid
but mother prevailed and my father
walked her up the aisle at St. Anne's in Tecumseh
and found most town folks of Stoney Point
were there anyway

Three weeks before my own wedding
my sister miscarried, but still waltzed
straight up the aisle of Annunciation
like the perfect July bride's maid beaming
for all the world to see

A Great Aunt Going Home

I now wish I had never gone that day
to join the family in moving a coffin
that belonged to a great aunt buried
alongside the Thames River
where grave sites were suffering erosion

It was noon, and we saw the diggers lift
her broken coffin from the ground
setting it down before loading it in a truck
to bring to the cemetery in Stoney Point

That's when my sister asked if we might open it

I turned away, fixing my attention instead
on that flat chalky-white headstone
that lay nearby bearing her name

then heard the men fidgeting with the coffin
partly ruined and split from water damage
— all that was left was a shroud
of black lace, a pewter cross
a mother-of-pearl hair comb, holy cards
bits of teeth and a tangle of red hair

Honeymoon Ride to Niagara Falls, July 1936

The hottest of summers, 111 degrees
with crops wilting and steel rail lines
and bridge girders twisting, and sidewalks
buckling and fruit baking on the trees
By Monday when we married, it started
to cool, and I could feel wind drifting in
through the open church windows

By day's end, with all the celebrations
and picture taking and dancing
I was so tired from smiling that when
I climbed into his car, my shoulders drooped
and I slumped back and shut my eyes for a moment
and smiled again because
someone was knocking on the window
— my sister Rose, blowing me a kiss
as my husband and I were off

His shiny 1934 Ford five-window coupe
swerving out of the farmyard to the dirt road
that led away from the lake
our bags packed and I remembered
leaving my wedding dress on the bed
upstairs at the farmhouse and
how my sister struggled to fit into it
but could not slip it past her waist
the two of us laughing so hard
we fell on the bed
nearly busting the bedsprings

all the while my husband waited downstairs
but now we were off to Niagara Falls
wending our way to King's Highway #3
windows down and windy as we sped along

It was still light out this late in the day
a razor-thin crescent moon hovered
over the barn and the tall black walnut trees
both sun and moon in the July sky
like distant cousins greeting one another

I studied him — square jaw, hair slicked back
a handsome smile talking non-stop
cigarette bobbing up and down like a baton
I'm not sure I really heard anything he said
—so happy I was to finally leave
everything behind

The Alvin, 1936

We moved in on a humid morning
at the beginning of August 1936 —
our first place, the three-storey brick
Alvin Apartments at 296 Pitt Street West

the lovely Art Deco archway
and wide solid wooden stairs that brought us
to the third floor, and it was there I spent
hours unpacking boxes, painting kitchen
cupboards, scrubbing floors, setting up
our life together downtown

occasionally pausing to daydream over
the neglected apple orchard across the street
or stare at the *Windsor Daily Star* building
watching the open trucks edging
out of the garages in the afternoon
with young newsboys, jumpers riding in the back

or much later, I'd see the *Star's* lights burning
all night on the second-floor newsroom
and wonder about the stories they made
the images they dreamed

My husband gone all day, driving to
Ford City early morning to work at the plant
and returning at suppertime
routinely reaching into the icebox for a beer
before taking off his coat, settling down
talking a mile-a-minute about his day
rarely wondering what I'd been up to

The place was clean, supper set out
and I'd sit with him, my bony elbows on the table
still wearing an apron, leaning in and listening
all about his bosses, troubles at the plant
everything under the sun, and more
and I don't think he ever once
noticed I'd put on lipstick
from the five-and-dime

Birth on Albert Road, 1937

We didn't stay long
renting the apartment downtown —
finally found a second-floor flat on Albert Road
a stone's throw from the plant
so my husband could run home at lunch
and his bosses laughed about that
for it wasn't long before I was pregnant

I started to show in November
and he was so proud, bragging to everyone
he was going to have a son
though silently I hoped for a little girl

Each night down below us we heard
the landlord's wife — an opera singer rehearsing
for a Detroit vaudeville act involving a troupe
of dancers, acrobats, jugglers, magicians
minstrels and impersonators
her voice reverberating trumpet-like
with a cutting edge that kept us awake

Over the next two years one way or another
we made it work waiting it out because
my husband was building a house
and our first born, a boy, arrived in June 1937
on the very day when all the talk in town
was not of him but of King Edward VIII
marrying the divorcee Wallis Simpson
at a Chateau de Conde in France

When the War Started

The war had started in September
and I feared my husband would join
the troops, sail overseas, and leave me
with two little ones, maybe perish in a trench
fighting a cause he could never explain

His younger brother was already in training
and neighbours were signing up daily —
a world plummeting into patriotism and zeal
and he wouldn't talk about it
so I rode a bus downtown one afternoon
to the recruitment office, two toddlers in hand
and I wanted to know if they were going
to take my husband from me, send him
to the front lines, send him to his death
and then what would I do? I was expecting —

and the man said he didn't know, couldn't say
spoke about duty, about putting an end to evil
but I had stopped listening, mesmerized instead
by the Union Jack pinned to the wall behind him
imagined long days and nights
waiting up, alone, worried

As it turned out, my husband wound up
working in a munitions plant feeding the war effort
and a few days before Christmas I lost the child
the late afternoon light fading —
and we sent for the doctor

and when it was done the doctor told my husband
what to do, and dutifully he gently placed the stillborn
in a threadbare towel, and I never asked
if it was a girl — I wanted a daughter

I lay exhausted and alone
and heard my husband nearby
disposing of the fetus in the coal furnace

George Avenue, December 1940

That day in December, the young
farm girls from Stoney Point
gathered in the house on George Avenue
to take care of my two youngest sons
while I gave birth to a third —

It was a good thing it happened then
— a couple of weeks later
winter storms had ground everything
to a standstill and the papers said "the ice
was as thick as a person's wrist" covering
telephone wires, trees and railway tracks
and nobody was left to help out
because the war was in full bloom
and the men were shipping out

In the midst of mounting labour pains
and whatever moaning he had heard
my oldest boy — not quite three —
slipped quietly into my bedroom
for a brief moment when I was alone
and before the girls came to pull him
away and back to his brother

he had climbed up and nuzzled close to me
and I put an arm around him
told him to put his hands over his ears
and told him not to worry
— it would all be over soon

The Suitcase

For years, it sat empty in the closet
under the stairs — that small suitcase
striped in gold and brown with rust trim
the one my sister gave me
as a wedding present, and I took it
on my honeymoon to Niagara Falls
the only place I ever used it —

I wasn't ever going anywhere soon

My mother warned me to keep it
A lady might need a way out

Chasing the Tornado, June 1946

I saw automobiles twist and spin
about in the air above wind-swept streets
a city bus, and bicycles wildly engulfed by the
black massive specter that sped ahead of us
this funnel cloud powerful and wicked
growing in immensity and looping a reckless path
though streets and backyards and open fields

and I watched my husband, still sporting a bowtie
from work, sleeves rolled up to the elbows
cigarette in the hand wildly, intently, but calmly
steer the car in pursuit and I wondered why
he packed all of us, our four sons
his own mom and dad and me pregnant
with my fifth son and I turned for an instant

to spy my oldest boy in the back seat staring
out the side vented window, his dark curly hair
falling over his forehead, gaping eyes large and scared
and I said *Don't worry, your father knows what he is doing*
but I didn't believe it for a moment feeling the whole
weight of the car swerving in and around the debris-laden
wake of this black ghost that led us on a wild mad chase

saw it devour trees, telephone poles and mangled wires
and rooftops ripped and whipped into the spinning
firmament and I shut my eyes, lips trembling in prayer
words tumbling out but swallowed up in the thunder
of wind and shouting, then opened my eyes to my husband
laughing and marveling at the ghost as it spun across
an open field, leaping and vanishing into an open sky

To be Opened Later, Winter 1947

It was a chilly winter day at the end of February
that I snipped a curl of blond hair from
my baby boy's head — and I slipped it
into a small envelope that I placed carefully
into a top dresser drawer, and hoped

in that moment he might come across it
might find it one day among all that we leave
behind, might spot it among boxes of
photographs and holy cards, might never know
the story from that winter day, sleet pelting

the windows, and trees bending in the cold wind
and the sky blackening as the day wore on
and my boy tossed and tossed with a fever
and I soothed him to sleep, sang to him
softly and easily, and watched the curl

twist on his damp forehead, and felt him
tumble into a dream, and in all the brilliance
of that fever, I trimmed that curl and
tucked it away, delicately edging it into
a crisp envelope like a lost apostrophe

Family Portrait, Belle Isle, Detroit 1949

We were all there getting ready to pile into
the sprawling four-door Plymouth Sedan on
a June afternoon on Belle Isle, picnic baskets
packed away in the trunk, all set to depart and
drive back across the border through the Tunnel
when my husband ordered us all to stand
and pose for this picture, and he held up

a brand-new Brownie Target Six-20, sun over
his shoulder, all the while shouting instructions
and pointing behind him at the late day sun streaming
through the red oaks on the island, and madly
recited guidelines verbatim from Eastman Kodak
on how best to take a picture, and that meant
keeping the sun over the right shoulder

and there — all of us queued up, annoyed
and struggling to look natural, and my three-year-old
whimpered about the sun burning holes in his eyes
right down to its sockets if he didn't soon shut them
— and my husband again started up
with the Brownie litany about this black box
likening it to the magical workings of the human eye

its lens resembling the eye's lens, its shutter, the eyelid
and the film resembling the retina *Stay still now! Don't
move now! Look right at the camera...*and my husband seemed
forever peering down into the viewfinder, backing up
and backing up to get us all in and I feared he might run
right up into a tree and we were all smiles except
for my littlest one lost in a daydream with his eyes on fire

Dresses in Our Closet, 1949

I could easily count the number of dresses
I owned — I had six, and that included
my wedding dress that was safely tucked away
in a stiff but elegant cardboard box
lined with mothballs —

I stored the box at the back of the only closet
in our bedroom — and prayed
a daughter might wear it
but I had five boys, no girls yet

Those cotton dresses hung to one side
of my husband's suits — he had three
and five white shirts I washed
and ironed every Saturday

Five cotton print dresses, my favourite
the "swirl" or wraparound that buttoned
at the middle, a pattern in red, and so comfortable
but I'd never wear it to church

Instead, I put on the one with the organdy collar
a rose colour, and it opened to the hem
had two pockets and two skirt pleats —
I wore that almost every Sunday

I promised myself I might
try my hand at making one of the gord skirts
with large patch pockets with detailed top stitching
but I wasn't going anywhere
— and there was no time with my young sons

One afternoon passing C.H. Smith's Department Store
I spotted a smart spun rayon plaid dress — it was
in the window display, and it had two rows
of green buttons, slit pockets and a darling collar
and a shirring under-waistline that draped
the dress so full and light —

I dreamed of dancing at Thomas's Inn on the river
but we never ever went there

but Smith's had my size, and I slipped into the dress
that very afternoon, and I must confess
how much I wanted this but dared not ask
— I thought maybe I could make it
but I had no idea where I'd wear it
maybe at church, maybe at Christmas
at a baptism

Here it was, right after the war
It sold for $4.98, all my grocery money

Welcome to my closet

Joe Louis: On the Road, Winter 1950

I spotted him — this tall black man jogging
past the house at dawn, straight along
the table-top flat road as if he was seemingly
going to run right off the face of the earth

and every day the same and once when
I was coming back from the barn, he waved
and I nodded formally, and he smiled
and much later, mother told me she knew him

and so, did I, if ever I paid any attention
to the world all around me — the troubles
that were just around the corner
but what about the radio broadcasts

of his fights and *Don't you know Joe Louis*
and another time when I was making my way to
collect eggs I spotted him silhouetted and running
the morning sun rising like a fist

over the open flat November fields, and my father
later said he spotted his Cadillac parked down
near the lake where he was training for a come-back —
that's the man on the windy road running

for all its worth to be the champion again
and I can't say that I knew him at all
or ever saw him again but that night
right after New Year's we gathered around

tuned into the fight on the radio
from Detroit's Olympia and he was
his old self swaggering and confident
blow after blow and you could feel it

in the sound, the crowd rising to their feet
in the glare of the old hockey arena
  — hometown for this man itching for a shot
at the next hero, the next legend to step up

Near Lighthouse Cove

The wind and rain just beginning
and so I hurried out to the yard —
to the sagging clothesline of white sheets
billowing out in the cool spring
in a day so dreary and gray

the kind of afternoon that reminded me
of my aunt, now old and forgetful
and the stories she wove in the clapboard
place near Lighthouse Cove
when I'd sit and listen and drink

a cup of tea, feeling darkness filling
the room as she spoke of things
she had done, tales I had heard before
from cousins and neighbours even
itinerant farmhands

most I was assured were entirely made up
but often as I walked back from her place
following ditch-lined farm roads
under a sky of rolling gloomy clouds
I couldn't help but scan the fields

and turn to look at the solitary barn
where one spring day on a Sunday
when she was 16 and stayed home while
everyone was at Mass, how she knelt
on the ground and hurriedly wrapped the fetus

she had miscarried, wrapped it in a blanket
and buried it in a shallow grave and if
I wanted, I could make my way there now
and find it, and if I did, would I tell her
if it was a son or daughter?

A Girl

The priest at Stoney Point said
I ought to wait a little longer
between children — I was pregnant
one right after another, miscarried once
but gave birth to three sons
in four years

I wanted a girl

The priest said my boys
could be priests — *consider it a blessing*
a sure sign I ought to wait, ought
to see God's plan unfold

I told him God had better deliver me a girl

When the World is Normal

I fell asleep, I think, and found myself
returning to that house in Riverside
on a dare, tumbling into a bewitching dream
and trembling as I climbed three steps
from the screen door to the kitchen

and they were all there moving in a blur
through a summer day in June
scent of lilacs just outside the windows
and I was wearing a satin flowered dress
my husband sporting a red bowtie

cigarette cupped in his hand at his side
and my oldest boy scooping ice cream
from a container on the counter
and the youngest reaching to get a good look
— the others on the verandah

It was maybe 1955 and the radio news
told me of Israel attacking Gaza
and the Chicago Cubs sending Sammy Jones
to the mound and pitching a no-hitter
against the Pirates

and a race car in Le Mans, France
swerving out of control and crashing
into the stands of spectators
killing 82 people
and I was there for only a few minutes

and nothing and everything seemed right
absolutely normal, an ordinary day in spring
when the sky was blue and the world
was falling apart as it should

Birthday Party, July 1956

The neighbourhood girls gathered
in the backyard in Riverside — a hot July day
party dresses, lemonade, and chocolate cake
and coloured streamers draped across the rooms
and backyard games and radio music
and, much later, front porch picture-taking
and my six-year-old was basking in the attention

just as I imagined this radiant day following
America's 4th of July, my dearest dream
of all, a birthday party, a first in our house
of five sons — and you can spot them at
the edges of the Brownie pictures, my boys,
bewildered by all the fuss, a cake was all

they ever got, especially two of my sons sharing
the same birthday — one cake for both but
no one cared, for them it was the rush from
a summer's screen door to the open street to the side
building lots, this scramble to freedom, away and
be gone was all they wanted, but for my girl

and her friends, it was a moment to soar and put
on party hats and squirm in dining room chairs
and pull down the blinds to keep the heat of July
at bay, and soon the late day darkness softened
and mellowed with lit candles and shrill voices
of eight little girls now rising and it was all brought

back home — that promise in my own childhood
of no birthdays, of no one taking notice, of waking

to a morning like any other day — farm chores
and cooking and schoolwork, but here we were
with a daughter like me, all lightness and laughter
on a perfect day in a room alive with innocence

The Young Boy and the Piano

The piano never took up space —
it was a part of our life though
neither my husband nor I could play
Still, I made sure each of my five sons
and two daughters learned, and no matter

where I was in the house, I heard them
running through the scales or playing waltzes
and soon I'd sit with my youngest boy
and remind him Mozart was playing at
the age of three, and I'd take hold of his hands

and ask if he could place five fingers
on five adjacent white keys, and knew this
to be a stretch for a five-year-old but if he could
he had a chance be the next Mozart,
and I'd watch his left hand slowly yawn

and reach for those ivory keys and his smile too
widened, and soon day after day he would practice
in the afternoons alone in the living room
and it never bothered me that he fractured
the simplest of tunes, never bothered me

that it was far from perfect — it was the sound
of someone seeking perfection, finding his way
maybe believing the story and hearing the silence
awaken that soft glimmering afternoon light
just beneath the pulled down blinds

Dear Ann Landers, Summer 1956

I had just turned 40 and though we never
went anywhere except for Sunday Mass
whenever I was introduced it was always the same
This is the wife, never my name
and I said nothing — I kept it to myself

till that afternoon when *The Star* arrived
and I read *Ask Ann Landers,* and a young wife
like me had written in, wondering if
it was rude to be introduced as *The Wife* —

and Ann wrote it was high time
her husband ought to recognize
she had a name, an identity, that
she was a living, breathing woman

I waited till after supper, handed him a beer
and the paper — opened to *Ann Landers*

Read this, and tell me what you think

Then I waited and it seemed forever
— I heard him slam down the paper
on the foot stool, and stand up
and head for the door —
saying nothing at all

For hours, he was gone —
and when he pulled into the driveway
it was late, and the first thing he did
coming into the house was light a cigarette

and for the longest time stood
staring down at his shoes, then looked up
straight into my eyes, and nodded

That's all it took

The Day My Mother Died, 1957

I wore only a wool sweater
overtop the house dress to step out
that crisp March morning
to do the chores and collect eggs
and my mother lay dead in the farmhouse
waiting for the funeral home fellow

and I left my half brother and sister
with my father who never seemed
to stir from the rocking chair
back and forth, back and forth
face silent and fixed on furrowed empty fields
and I followed the muddied path down

to the clapboard henhouse
sun lazily stretching awake
I heard the cold rain that day tapping
on the tin roof of the narrow hen house
and my frigid hands ever familiar, slipped
under and scooped up the warm eggs

all done with a soothing voice
though I knew none of these ladies
not like when I was a young girl
and they all had names
and we had our favourites
but this was our first hello

and not a blemish of brooding in the nest
I spoke about mother and how
she wouldn't be coming anymore

— they'd never see her graceful and quiet
and routinely moving shape stepping
in and among them, cheering them on

during the darkest cold days of winter
thanking each one individually
I knew I wouldn't be returning
so, I'd never get to know them
yet I promised the hired hand might come
or my uncle's teenage son, someone

so not to worry, spring was starting up
and as I turned to leave to unlatch the flimsy
wooden door I turned again to address them
— holding up a basket of a dozen brown eggs
thanking them all in their nesting boxes
and saying *You've done well today, girls!*

Time Alone, 1957

Ironing shirts gave me a step away
a moment alone, strangely
reminding me what it was like at Mass
lost in solitary prayer, alone though surrounded
by others, still one with God and now
I was one with a shirt — yes, ironing

my husband's white shirts to wear
at the factory, pressed crisp and perfect
routinely ironing them inside out
and could do each easily in 90 seconds
but I never rushed, lolled about
listening to Arthur Godfrey on the radio

five shirts a week, Friday morning
ironing board standing like a trained puppy
in the middle of the room amid the chaos
the comings and goings but the moment
that thunders back was that day in April 1945
— President Roosevelt's funeral

first time I ever heard Arthur Godfrey live
a broadcast of the funeral procession
speaking like a best friend, down-to-earth
heart-felt easy tone, emotional, solemn
I could see the moment clearly, sense it swell
in my chest, and feel its intimate hurt

so beguiled by the voice and radio sound
of that day, it was as if my hands were moving
now on their own, pressing and lifting and

and sliding and folding the shirts each one
my hands mirroring the rhythm of that voice
and 90 seconds soon became an hour

My Uncle, the Catholic Priest

His picture rested for years on the upright piano
at home just above where each of my boys
and two daughters practiced their scales —
an endless stream filtering throughout
the house and past the screen door

and I never believed the stories about him
— he was my mother's brother
a bespectacled priest who had to run off
to Montréal to be ordained because
the London bishop warned him

that even if he could manage to speak
a perfect sentence in English he'd still
never survive the seminary, and certainly would
never be ordained — he was a boy, born on
a Stoney Point farm, but was never much

interested in its demands — instead lazed away
long afternoons in an upstairs farmhouse room
or fell asleep in the barn's hayloft reading
The Lives of the Saints, dreaming of life in the church
the comfort of a rectory, farm girls cooking

and cleaning for him, afternoons taken up
perusing church theology or Friday nights
listening to radio broadcasts of fights from
Madison Square Gardens and Sunday mornings
telling parishioners how best to get to Heaven

I never believed the stories about how
he scooped up all the family farms
in the midst of the Depression, let his brothers
and cousins live there and work the land and pay
him with eggs and corn and tomatoes but when

times changed, he'd ask for a new car, a trip
to Quebec, gifts for his housekeeper, but he'd
never let them off the hook — they kept paying
and soon he bought a house near Assumption
University and at dusk would step out and stroll

through the nearby graveyard where lay many old friends
and some say he'd and smile and scoff and croon about how
he had made out, how he snubbed the iron will
of London's bishop, how he had his own parish
and was really an itinerant Catholic priest working

the back streets of nearby Detroit and no one
had dominion over him on this side of the river
but I never quite believed the rumours
about his housekeeper who lived in his house
cooked his meals and washed his clothes

and was there for him to complain, there for him
when he died, and she was left the house, his library
the sprawling black Buick, and some say she was
blessed to inherit all the family farms that housed
his siblings, and why not, she was his wife

My Father's Wives

My father had three wives
— two after my mother passed away
and they both looked like her
and both were at her funeral
and both stopped by the wake
and passed by the chair
that he sat in, both eyeing him
both wanting his attention

But my father's blue eyes were dulled
by the day and the mourning over
the loss of my mother
He didn't notice

Instead he dreamt of a better time
memory taking him back
to when he first met her
at a late spring picnic

that day when he wore
a buttoned-up wool suit and tie
and kept running his broad hand over
his head, feeling the heat of the day

and it was my mother who stepped forward
and offered a handkerchief
and he smiled and nodded his thanks
and wiped his forehead, and
from that moment on, they grew close
and not long after, he proposed

My mother was 17, and she married him
four months after she turned 18
married at St. Anne's in Tecumseh
and they moved to a small farm on Highway #2
before buying 50 acres near the Lighthouse
two miles outside of Stoney Point

My father was never one for thinking out loud
and still possessed a courtly grace, and so
without fail each and every wedding anniversary
he found his way back from the fields
at the end of day, and stepped
into the big kitchen with the wood stove
and carefully bowed
as he slowly swept a bouquet
of spring flowers from behind his back

— blue eyes sparkling in the waning daylight
and maybe it was chasing that moment
in months following my mother's death
that he married, and once more
after his second wife's death

He seemed broken, alone and spent
— he knew there was no more to give

Wedding Dress

I saw my daughter upstairs
struggling in her bedroom
trying on my wedding dress
and we both laughed
when I caught her —
one arm entangled in the dress
she could barely fit into

I saw my other daughter
years later unlatching the cedar chest
in search of something else
and I showed her the dress
—she ignored me
so the dress remained there

until my granddaughter
one cool afternoon in June
emerged from the bedroom
wearing the dress

— she was maybe 16
and I watched her spin around
and around, and it made me think
of that day when I rode
with my father and mother
from the farm into Windsor
and we parked in front
of C.H. Smith's Department Store
where I met my sister
and we both tried on dresses

but my mother had already decided
thought this long gown of satin and lace
was the right one —
and on my way back to the farm
the stiff brown box with the dress
sat on my lap
till I carried it upstairs
and lifted it out to marvel
at its softness

I hung it on a curtain rod
in the west window of my room
and fell asleep only to wake
hours later to find
the shimmering dress
like an angel
hovering at the window
in the late afternoon light

The Painter's Dream

My husband was happiest
when he was painting, but had pretty well
given up on such dreams, instead pushed
any notions aside for the factory job
raising our children, putting food
on the table, going about making things
work out, knowing what it was like

during the Great Depression, and
that was fine, but when he retired and
started drinking, the ugliness surfaced
and, somehow, he knew there had
to be better choices, and so
he would descend the stairs
to the basement with the pool table

and arrange small white canvases
across its green veneer, and one by one
he would paint the lakes and skies
and islands of boyhood memory
and the hours would float away
and so would the anger and slowly
he was in love again with that dream

Reading Between the Lines

I'd watch my husband strain
to read the headlines — he was going blind
and no matter what I said, he was stubbornly proud
never once inviting me to take the paper
and read the stories out loud to him

He preferred to guess at the outcomes
the content, reading between the lines
speculating at the shapes of words
and what they might mean and for him
the world unfolded as he needed

I was alright with that for I knew
how his arms still found me in the
hollows and darkness of our years together
and that made all the difference as
his hands gently traced the shape of my face

The Barn

I was in my late 60's, the last time
I was at the farm, and I walked
with my half brother
passing the well and the rickety hen house
saw the barn that stood in front
of the Black Walnut grove —
most trees thinned out over the years

I wanted to climb up to the timbered
loft but my half brother warned me
it wasn't safe — there were huge gaps in the flooring
cautioned me about hitting my head
on the wooden support beams

I climbed the ladder, and at the top
no surprise but a snarl of a spider web
shimmering in radiant sunlight, and
I reached out, and swept much of it away
and stepped up to the loft

I wanted to see as a child, be that girl
who once paused in the quiet — counting
the stripes of afternoon light glowing over
a dusty floor strewn with bits of hay

I sat cross-legged on the floor, shut
my eyes, as in silent prayer, and heard the chirp
and whine of barn swallows, thought
I felt the thrust of wind so high up above

and below me was this perfectly spaced plan
of a house, clapboard buildings, tall grass in
the walnut grove, and the flat open land
that opened its grasp to the lake beyond

I was home

Last Will

When I pass
leave the dresses
hanging in the closet

They will remind you
that I am still there

Don't give them away

Acknowledgements

I never realized until much later just how much my mother's stories mirrored those of her favourite writer, Guy de Maupassant, who wrote about war, religion, madness, were-wolves, haunted villages, and life in 19th century France. As a boy, she read me the stories of this great French writer, and I have since gone back to read them myself. What fascinates me about his fiction is how things never turn out exactly as one believes they might. My mother's stories possessed that same element of surprise.

In putting this book together, I sought the assistance of two much older brothers, Paul and Ted, as well as my sister, Rosemary Weiler. The three clarified specific details behind my mother's stories, and sure, they may have embellished a little in the telling. Of course, my thanks to Micheline Maylor for her thoughtful preface, as well as insightful edits to the original manuscript. I am also grateful to both Heather McCardell and KC Santo for their suggestions and copyediting.

A video excerpt (https://www.youtube.com/watch?v=VxnpS0R48Us) by Taylor Campbell was produced in June 2020 for Youtube, with financial support from Cultural Affairs for the City of Windsor.

Meanwhile, the ornate famed picture of the ghostly great-grandmother still hangs in my house and, from time to time, it surprises us and topples to the floor. We gently put it back up each time and apologize.

About the Author

Marty Gervais is an award-winning journalist, poet, and photographer, and served as the City of Windsor's first Poet Laureate. In 1996, he was awarded the Milton Acorn People's Poetry Award for his Mosaic Press book, *Tearing Into A Summer Day*. This book also was granted the City of Windsor Mayor's Award for literature. In 1998, he won the prestigious Toronto's Harbourfront Festival Prize for his contributions to Canadian letters and to emerging writers. In 2003, Gervais was given the City of Windsor Mayor's Award for literature for *To Be Now: Selected Poems*, another Mosaic Press title. His most successful work, *The Rumrunners*, a book about the Prohibition period, was a Canadian bestseller and was on the top ten Globe and Mail bestseller list for non-fiction titles. Another book, *Seeds In The Wilderness*, stemmed from interviews Gervais conducted with such notable religious leaders as Mother Theresa, Bishop Desmond Tutu, Hans Kung, and Terry Waite.